# Christmas Tales

I Talk You Talk Press

# CONTENTS

# INTRODUCTION

In this book there are five short Christmas stories for learners of English.

# 1.  TWO SLICES OF CHRISTMAS CAKE

Kenta Kinoshita was a university student in Tokyo. He was in the first grade. It was his first year away from his family. His family lived very far away, in Sapporo, Hokkaido.

Our story starts just before Christmas, on 24th December.

Kenta was looking at a poster in the student cafeteria.

*---Student Christmas Party!! Sunday, 26th December at 7:00pm!!---*

Kenta's friend, Yoshi, saw him.

"Hey, Kenta! Are you going to the Christmas party?" asked Yoshi.

"I don't know," said Kenta.

Kenta wanted to go to the party, but there was a problem. He didn't have a girlfriend.

"Everyone is going to the party," said Yoshi. "I'm going with Yuka, Hiroshi is going with Asaka, and Gary is going with Chiemi."

"I see," said Kenta. "I'll think about it."

*All my friends have girlfriends,* he thought. *If I go to the party, I will be alone.*

After lunch, Kenta went to class. It was a small seminar and there were only five students. They were all talking about the party. Only one student wasn't talking about the party. That was Sarah, the student from Canada.

*Maybe she's not interested in the party,* thought Kenta. *But she doesn't speak Japanese very well. So she doesn't talk to the other students much. Christmas is a happy time, but she doesn't look happy.*

That night, Kenta went back to his student apartment. His apartment was on the university campus. He looked out of the window. It was snowing. He could see students outside. Some of them were having a snowball fight. Two girls were shouting, "Merry Christmas!"

*Yes, Merry Christmas,* thought Kenta. *It's Christmas tomorrow. What shall I do?*

Every Christmas, Kenta's mother baked a strawberry and cream cake for Christmas.

*I wish I was home in Sapporo,* he thought. *I want to eat my mother's strawberry and cream cake.*

Kenta got into bed.

*I'll go to the cake shop tomorrow. I'll buy a piece of cake for myself. Just for me,* he thought. Then he fell asleep.

The next evening, at about 6:00pm, Kenta finished studying in the library, and went to a cake shop in central Tokyo. There was a long line of people outside. He stood in the line and waited.

At last, he was near the front of the line. The people in front of him were ordering some cake.

"Two slices of strawberry cake please," said a man.

"Two slices of strawberry and cream tart please," said a woman.

*Everyone is ordering two slices of cake,* thought Kenta. *Everyone has a partner. I have to ask for just one slice. Cake for one person. I feel ashamed.*

"Yes sir? What would you like?" said the woman behind the counter.

"Er…one slice of strawberry and cream cake, please," said Kenta quietly.

"Pardon?" said the woman. "I'm sorry, I didn't hear you. Could you say that again please?"

Kenta felt his face turn red. People were looking at him.

"Er, two slices of strawberry and cream cake please," he said.

"Two slices?" asked the woman.

"Yes," said Kenta.

The woman put two slices of cake into a box and gave it to Kenta. He gave her the money.

There was an older woman behind Kenta.

"I think your girlfriend will enjoy that cake," said the woman, smiling. "It looks delicious."

Kenta smiled. Then, he walked out of the cake shop.

Kenta was walking back to his apartment. He walked past restaurants. There were many couples in the restaurants.

*They look happy,* he thought. He walked along the river. There were Christmas lights on the buildings on the other side of the river. It was snowing a little, but Kenta was walking, so he felt warm.

Kenta saw someone sitting on a bench next to the river. It was dark, so he couldn't see very well.

*Who's that? It's a foreign woman,* he thought. The woman was looking at the Christmas lights across the river.

Then, he heard a noise. It sounded like the woman was crying.

*Is she crying?* he thought.

He got closer.

*It's Sarah! From Canada! But, why is she crying?*

He stopped walking.

*What should I do?* he thought. *Should I say something?*

Kenta started to feel nervous. *Sarah's Japanese is not very good. And my English is not good, but she is crying. I should say something,* he thought.

He took a deep breath.

"Sarah?" he said.

Sarah turned around and looked at him.

"Kenta?" she said.

"Yes. It's Kenta. Are you OK?"

Sarah smiled. "Yes, I'm OK," she said.

"But you are crying," said Kenta. "You don't look OK."

"I'm feeling homesick," said Sarah. "It's Christmas. I want to be with my family. But I am here. Alone."

"I see," said Kenta. "That's too bad."

"Yeah. But how about you, Kenta? Are you going somewhere?"

"No, I just went shopping," said Kenta.

"What did you buy?" asked Sarah.

Kenta looked at the cake box.

"Some Christmas cake," he said.

"You eat Christmas cake?" asked Sarah.

"Every year my mother made Christmas cake for me. But this year, I am far from my home. I felt homesick. So, I bought some Christmas cake."

"For you and your girlfriend?"

"No, just for me," said Kenta. "I don't have a girlfriend. But…"

He opened the box.

"I have two slices. Do you want one?"

Sarah smiled. "I would love one, thank you."

"Here you are," said Kenta. He gave her a slice of cake.

They ate the cake. It was delicious.

"Kenta, I don't understand. Why did you buy two slices of cake?" asked Sarah.

Kenta looked at the floor. "Well, I wanted to buy one slice, but in the shop, all the other people were buying two slices, to eat with their boyfriend or girlfriend. I didn't want to say 'one slice'," said Kenta.

Sarah laughed. "Oh Kenta, that's so cute."

Kenta felt his face go red. *Cute? She thinks I'm cute?* he thought.

"But I'm glad you bought two slices. I enjoyed it very much. And I feel better. Thank you," said Sarah.

"You're welcome," said Kenta.

They finished eating the cake. Kenta closed the cake box. "It's cold. Shall we go back to the campus?" he said.

Sarah and Kenta walked back to the campus. They talked about Canada and Hokkaido and about homesickness.

Kenta enjoyed talking to Sarah. And he was pleased because he was speaking English very well.

The next day, Kenta woke up.

*It's the day of the Christmas party,* he thought. *I'll go to the library. Then, tonight I'll watch a movie in my room. All my friends will be at the party, so we can't do anything together tonight.*

Kenta picked up his bag of textbooks and walked out of his apartment. In the apartment lobby, he saw something in his mailbox.

*What's that?* he thought.

He opened the mailbox. There was a pink envelope. He opened it.

It was a letter in English. He read it.

*---Dear Kenta,*

*Thank you for the cake yesterday. I was very sad and homesick, but after talking to you, I felt better. And the cake was delicious. It was very kind of you to give me a slice of your cake.*

*I would like to say thank you. I have a small present for you. Are you going to the party tonight? If you are going to the party, can we go together? Here is my mobile phone number and e-mail address. Please contact me if you would like to go to the party with me. From Sarah. ----*

Kenta smiled. *I'm glad I bought two slices of cake yesterday,* he thought.

"Good morning Kenta!"

He turned around. It was Yoshi. He was walking out of his apartment.

"Good morning Yoshi."

"So, Kenta, are you going to the party tonight or not?" asked Yoshi.

"Yes, of course, I'm going to the party," said Kenta, smiling. "Of course!"

# 2.  A MAKEOVER FOR CHRISTMAS

It's Monday, and it's morning coffee break at work. My friend Maddy and I are standing next to the coffee machine. We are talking. Drew Lawrence, the most handsome guy in the office, walks over to us. He stops.

"Are you two doing anything on Saturday night? I'm having a Christmas party," he says.

"No. Nothing special," says Maddy. "We can come, can't we Kirstie?"

I say yes.

"Great," he smiles. "I'll give you my address later." He walks away. Maddy and I look at each other.

"He invited us to the party because he likes you," says Maddy.

"No, he likes you. Anyway, we're going to a party! At his house!"

Maddy and I talk about it all week.

"What shall we wear?" asks Maddy. This is a very important question. Maddy is lucky. She's small. She has dark curly hair. She's very pretty. She looks good in any kind of clothes. I am tall and thin. I look good in jeans, but I don't look good in skirts. So I never wear them.

We don't have much money, but we want something new to wear to the party. We go out every day at lunchtime and look in the shops.

I find a red shirt in a bargain box. I will wear my best black trousers and my black boots.

Maddy buys a silver dress. It's very short, but she says, "No problem. I'll wear leggings underneath it."

On Friday, Maddy and I eat lunch in the work cafeteria. Maddy has a magazine.

"Look, Kirstie," she says. "This fashion model looks like you."

She shows me a picture. The model is beautiful.

"No, I don't look like her. But look at her hair. It's wonderful." The model's hair is a mixture of brown and dark blonde.

"You will look like her if you change your hair colour," says Maddy.

"I'd like to change my hair colour. But I don't have enough money to go to the hairdressers."

Maddy has a great idea. "I'll do it for you. We'll buy some hair colour. I'm sure it is easy."

So after work we go out to do some more shopping. Maddy hates her eyelashes. She thinks they are too short. She wants to buy false eyelashes to wear to the party. We go to the department store. The cheapest false eyelashes are 10 pounds. Maddy doesn't have enough money. The hair colour kits are expensive too.

"Let's go to the discount shop," says Maddy. "Everything is cheap there."

The discount shop sells many different things. Everything is very, very cheap. We buy false eyelashes and a hair colour kit. We are very excited.

Early on Saturday, I go to Maddy's home. I love visiting Maddy. She has two younger brothers. They are always laughing and telling jokes. It's a very cheerful house. The boys are decorating the Christmas tree. They have boxes of decorations and strings of lights all over the floor.

"Stay out of the bathroom!" Maddy tells her brothers. "Kirstie and I will be busy. We are making ourselves beautiful."

Maddy takes a chair into the bathroom. "Sit down," she says. She looks at the box of hair colour. I feel nervous. "Maddy," I say. "I don't think this is a good idea!"

"Of course it's a good idea. We put this rubber cap on your head. It's like a swimming cap, but it has holes in it. There's a plastic hook in the box. I use the hook and pull some of your hair through these holes. I put the hair colour on. You sit and wait for fifteen minutes. Then you wash your hair. Simple!"

"OK," I say. "Do it!"

It takes Maddy a long time but finally she is finished. "Now we wait fifteen minutes," she says. "I'm going to try my false eyelashes."

She opens the box. "I need glue. There's no glue in the box. I'll go and find some."

She goes away and comes back with a tube of glue and a magazine. "I found some glue in my brothers' room. They are always making models. Here's a magazine. Don't talk to me. I need to concentrate."

I read the magazine. Maddy is sitting at the bathroom mirror.

After a while, I ask Maddy, "Is it fifteen minutes yet? Can you check? It must be time to wash this hair colour off."

Maddy answers. "Uh, sorry Kirstie. I can't look at the clock right now. I seem to have a small problem."

I turn around to look at her. She has beautiful long eyelashes. But her eyes are closed.

"They look great! Open your eyes so I can see you properly," I say.

"Well, that's the problem. I can't."

"What?"

"I can't open my eyes! The glue has stuck my top eyelashes, my bottom eyelashes and the false eyelashes together. Maybe I used too much."

"Maybe it was the wrong glue!'

I forget about my hair. I jump up to help Maddy. We try hot water. We try soap. We try hair shampoo. Nothing works. Maddy's eyes are glued shut.

"What are we going to do?" I ask Maddy.

"I'll have to pull the false eyelashes off. Maybe that will work."

"That will hurt," I tell Maddy.

"I know, but I have to do it. I can't see."

Maddy takes one end of the false eye lashes and pulls very hard. "Ouch!" she shouts.

Then she pulls the other ones off. "Oooh!" she shouts again.

Maddy's brothers hear the noise. They come running into the bathroom.

"Is everything OK?" asks Colin. He's the eldest.

Maddy points to her eyes. They are very red. There are tears running down her face.

"Oh no," says Colin.

"Uh, Maddy," says Mark.

"Yes?" she replies.

"You have no eyelashes."

Maddy looks in the mirror. "Oh no!"

It's true. When Maddy pulled off the false eyelashes, all her natural eyelashes came off too. She looks strange.

Maddy and I look at each other. "What am I going to do? I can't go to a party looking like this!" she cries.

"Wear sunglasses," says Mark, laughing.

Mark is joking, but Maddy is serious. "I don't have any sunglasses."

"We'll find you some," says Colin.

The boys walk out the bathroom, but then Mark stops.

"I love your hair colour, Kirstie. It's perfect for Christmas."

"Oh, thank you, Mark," I say. I'm pleased.

Then I see Maddy's face. She is looking at my head, and she looks shocked.

She picks up the clock and looks at it. "Forty five minutes," she says quietly. "The instructions said fifteen minutes."

Now I run to the mirror. I still have the rubber cap on my head. The hair I can see is green. Not greenish-brown, or brownish-green. Bright green.

"Quick," says Maddy. "I'll wash it. Maybe the colour will come out."

Maddy shampoos my hair three times, but the colour doesn't change. I still have dark blonde hair with green stripes in it.

"I'll blow dry it," says Maddy. "Maybe it won't look so bad then."

It's getting late. I don't want to go to the party, but Maddy wants to go. She really likes Drew Lawrence.

"Please come, Kirstie," says Maddy. "I'm so sorry about your hair. But it doesn't look so bad. It's perfect for a Christmas party."

"Oh, OK," I say.

We get dressed. I have my new red shirt. Maddy looks beautiful in her short silver dress but her eyes are still very red and puffy.

We go to the living room. The boys have finished the tree. It looks beautiful. They are laughing a lot. Colin is holding something behind his back.

"We found you some sunglasses, Maddy. And, because it's Christmas, we've decorated them for you," he said.

He shows Maddy the sunglasses. They are very big joke sunglasses. Colin and Mark have put small Christmas lights around the frames.

"Look, Maddy!" Colin puts the sunglasses on. A cord hangs down behind his ear. At the end of the cord is a small battery pack. He turns on the switch and the lights flash on and off.

I feel sorry for Maddy, but the glasses are very funny. I laugh.

"And for you!" Mark turns to me. "Your hair looks like a tree, so you need decorations!"

The boys have used left-over decorations to make me a hat. It has strings of gold beads, red and green balls and a star on top. The star has a light in it, and it also flashes on and off.

"Try them on!" the boys say. Maddy puts on the sunglasses and I put on the hat. The boys cannot stop laughing. I look at Maddy in the sunglasses, she looks at me wearing the hat, and we start laughing too.

"You are so beautiful!" the boys tell us.

"Let's go to the party," I say. "We look stupid and everyone will laugh at us, but maybe there will be some nice food."

We go to the party. We are a big success. We have a great time. Everyone loves our Christmas party wear.

"Wow," says Drew Lawrence. "I'm so pleased I invited you. All the guys here want to dance with you. You are always so quiet at work, but tonight you are so much fun. I will tell everyone in the office about you. They will be very surprised."

Maddy and I look at each other. *It's Saturday night, and we are a big success,* I think. *But what about work on Monday morning? I will have to wear a hat, and Maddy will have to find some normal sunglasses.*

Maddy always knows what I am thinking.

"Never mind," she says quietly. "Monday is Monday. At least we are beautiful tonight!"

## 3.  SECRET SANTA

Do you know about 'Secret Santa'? Many offices and factories play Secret Santa before Christmas. All the workers in the office or factory write their names on a piece of paper. Then, they put the names into a box. Each person takes a piece of paper. They have to buy a present for that person. They wrap the present, and on the day of the Christmas party, they take the present to the office or factory. So everyone gets one present.

This is a story about Secret Santa in a factory in Newcastle, in northern England.

It was lunchtime at the factory. Everyone was sitting in the staff room. They were eating their lunch.

"It's Secret Santa time everyone," said Rosie, the manager. She gave everyone a small piece of paper. "Write your name on the paper and put it in this box."

*Oh no,* thought Adam. *I hate Secret Santa.*

Adam didn't have any friends in the factory. He was very shy. No one spoke to him. The other workers liked going out to parties and pubs. They went drinking every Friday night after work. Adam didn't like going out. He couldn't talk to people easily.

The other workers often said, "Adam is strange. He doesn't talk. He doesn't have any friends. He doesn't like drinking. He's different from us."

Every year, for Secret Santa, Adam got socks. Cheap black socks from the one pound shop. The other workers got perfume, whisky or DVDs. But he only got socks.

Adam wrote his name on the piece of paper and put it in the box.
On the next table, he heard Emma and Jill talking.

"I hope I don't get Adam," said Emma.

"If you do, just get him some black socks," said Jill, quietly. "He's boring."

Bob, a new worker, was sitting at the same table. Bob was older than the other workers.

"Jill, that's not nice. Adam heard you," said Bob to Jill.

"I don't care," said Jill. She looked at Adam. "Hey, Adam, what do you want for Christmas? Black socks?" Jill and Emma started laughing.

Bob looked at Adam. Adam didn't say anything. He ate his ham and cheese sandwiches and drank his tea.

Everyone put their names in the box. Rosie shook the box.

"OK everyone," she said. "Take a name."

Everyone took a name from the box.

"Our Christmas lunch party is 23rd December. So bring the presents then."

She looked at the clock. "It's one o'clock. Time to go back to work!"

Everyone stood up and went to the factory floor. Bob was walking behind Emma and Jill.

"Who did you get?" asked Emma.

"I got Sue," said Jill. "How about you?"

"I got Adam," said Emma.

Jill started laughing. "Black socks?" she said.

"Well, socks are cheap, but I don't want to spend any money on Adam. Even one pound socks are too much!" said Emma.

"So what are you going to buy?" asked Jill.

"I don't know," said Emma. "Maybe I will get him an empty box! He will have a surprise when he opens it! No present! Just an empty box!"

Jill laughed. "That will be so funny! Maybe he will cry!"

"Emma," said Bob. "I'll have Adam. Here, you can have Cathy."

"No. I don't want to change. I want to get Adam an empty box."

"That's not nice, Emma," said Bob.

Emma and Jill laughed.

"So?" said Jill.

*These girls are not nice,* thought Bob. *I don't like working with them.*

That afternoon, Bob watched Adam. He was a quiet man. He worked very hard.

*If Emma gets him an empty box, he will be very sad and embarrassed. I have to do something. What can I do?* thought Bob. *Does Adam have any hobbies? Should I ask him? No, if I ask him, there will be no surprise on 23rd December.*

Then, Bob had an idea.

He saw Rosie, his manager. "Rosie, I don't feel well. Can I go to the toilet?" he asked.

"Can't you wait until break time?" asked Rosie.

"I can't. I really need to go to the toilet now," said Bob. "Please Rosie. I ate some chicken at the café near my house last night. Now I have a bad stomach."

"OK. But be very quick," said Rosie.

Bob ran upstairs. He didn't go to the toilet. He went to the staff room. Everyone's coats and bags were at the back of the staff room. He found Adam's coat and bag. He opened the bag. He saw Adam's lunch box and wallet. There was nothing else.

Then he noticed Adam's coat. There was something in the pocket. He looked in the pocket. It was an old personal CD player.

He opened the CD player. The CD was of a band called The Big Flowers.

*He likes The Big Flowers,* thought Bob. *My younger sister, Jane, likes The Big Flowers too. She's very shy. She doesn't have many friends. Maybe shy people like The Big Flowers. They are not so famous.*

He put the CD player back in Adam's pocket and went back to the factory floor.

Later that night, Bob looked at The Big Flowers' website.

"I don't believe it!" he shouted. The Big Flowers were playing a New Year concert in Newcastle. There were a few tickets left, but they were expensive.

*Maybe Adam already has a ticket,* he thought. *I'll ask him about his New Year plans tomorrow.*

The next day, Bob asked Adam about New Year.

"What are you doing at New Year Adam?" he asked.

"Nothing," said Adam. "I'm going to stay at home. How about you?"

"I'm going out with my girlfriend," said Bob.

"That's nice," said Adam. He looked very sad.

"Do you have a girlfriend Adam?" asked Bob.

"No, I don't. Girls don't like me. And I am too shy to find a girlfriend," said Adam.

"Some girls like shy men," said Bob.

"Maybe," said Adam. "But they don't like me."

Later that night, Bob made some phone calls.

*I hope my plan is successful,* he thought.

It was 8:00am on 23rd December. All the workers were putting the Secret Santa presents under the Christmas tree in the staff room.

Emma and Jill were laughing. Bob was watching them. Emma put a large box under the tree.

"That's a large box," said Dan. "Someone is lucky."

"Yes, someone is very lucky!" said Jill.

Emma and Jill laughed very loudly.

At 11:30, Bob said to Rosie, "Can I go to the toilet?"

"Again? Do you still have stomach problems?" asked Rosie.

"I'm sorry Rosie, but I have a very bad stomach-ache."

Rosie looked at him.

"Oh OK," she said. "But be quick!"

Bob ran up to the staff room. He took an envelope out of his coat pocket. He picked up the large box from under the tree.

It was very big, but it was very light. Very carefully, he opened the red wrapping paper and opened the box. It was empty. He put an envelope in the box and wrapped the box again.

At lunchtime, everyone walked into the staff room. Everyone had cakes and sweets for the Christmas party. They put them on a large table in the centre of the room, and everyone sat around the table. Rosie put some Christmas music on the large CD player in the corner, and everyone talked about their Christmas plans.

At 12:30, Rosie said, "OK! It's time for Secret Santa!"

Bob looked at Adam. Adam looked very sad.

Rosie looked at the names on the presents.

"This one is for you Bob," said Rosie.

"Thank you," he said. He opened it.

It was a small bottle of vodka. "Great! Thank you!" he said. "I'll drink this on Christmas morning!"

Everyone laughed.

Next was Cathy. She got some chocolates. Then Dan. He got a Star Wars DVD. Then Sue, then Jill, then Emma and Phil. Everyone was very happy with the presents.

"And this large box is for Adam," said Rosie.

Emma and Jill started to laugh quietly.

"That's a big box. What's in it?" said Jill.

"Maybe it's socks?" said Emma. They laughed again.

Everyone was quiet. They all watched Adam open the box. Adam's face was red. Slowly, he opened the box.

"What's in it?" asked Jill again.

Adam took out the envelope. "It's an envelope," he said.

Emma and Jill looked at each other.

"What?" said Emma.

Adam opened the envelope. He took out two tickets.

"Oh! Two tickets to The Big Flowers concert!" said Adam, smiling.

"What?" said Emma and Jill together.

"Oh, thank you!" said Adam. "These tickets are expensive! They are too expensive for me to buy. But, who gave me these?"

No one said anything.

"Adam, that's a secret," said Rosie. "The game is called 'Secret Santa' because it's a secret."

Then Adam said, "Two tickets... Who will come to the concert with me?"

He looked around. No one said anything.

"My sister likes The Big Flowers," said Bob. "Shall I ask her? Maybe she can go."

Adam smiled. "Yes please. That's very kind of you."

"OK, that's it! Time to go back to work!" said Rosie.

Everyone started to tidy up. Bob went outside for a few minutes. Then, he came back.

"Adam, I just called my sister. She can go to the concert. She is looking forward to meeting you and going to the concert," he said.

Adam looked at Bob. "Thank you Bob," he said. "Merry Christmas."

"Merry Christmas Adam," said Bob. "And a Happy New Year."

# 4.  THE GINGERBREAD LADY

"Time for supper!" calls Suzanna.

Damon and Erica don't come.

Suzanna thinks it's strange. The children have been in Erica's room since they came home from school. Usually they are very hungry.

She goes to Erica's room. The two children are working at Erica's desk. Paints, paper, glue and glitter are spread all over the desk and the floor.

"What are you doing? It's time for supper," says Suzanna.

"Go away! It's a secret!" shouts Damon.

"Come and eat! Now!"

The children follow their mother to the kitchen.

Suzanna has cooked spaghetti and meatballs. It is the children's favourite, but they don't eat much.

"What's wrong?" asks Suzanna.

"I guess we ate too many cookies," says Erica.

"Cookies? What cookies?"

"The gingerbread lady gave us some cookies."

Suzanna is angry. "You know you must never take food from strangers!"

Erica is surprised. "She's not a stranger. She's the gingerbread lady. She lives in the gingerbread house. We talk to her all the time."

"Do you have any more of these cookies?"

"Some," says Damon. "She told us to keep them for Christmas, but they are so good we ate most of them."

"Get them now! Bring them to me," shouts Suzanna.

Damon goes to Erica's room and brings back a few cookies in a red paper bag.

Suzanna takes them from him and throws them in the garbage can.

"You listen to me! You must never talk to strangers. You must never talk to this woman again. Do you hear me?"

"But…" Damon wants to argue with his mother.

"No, Damon. Go to your room now!"

"You spoil everything!" says Damon. He goes to his room and closes the door very loudly.

Erica is still sitting at the table. She looks at Suzanna. "You are like a witch," she says. She stands up and goes to her room.

Suzanna sits down and puts her head in her hands. She feels very sorry for herself.

Suzanna's husband, Alan, is working in Saudi Arabia. He is an engineer. He cannot come home for Christmas. Suzanna and Alan hope to buy a house when he comes home. They are saving money. So Suzanna and the children are living in a cheap apartment. Suzanna is lonely. It is difficult for her to look after the children without support.

She cleans the kitchen and goes to say goodnight to the children. Damon's door is locked. She knocks and calls out, but Damon shouts, "Go away."

She goes to Erica's room. The door is not locked but when Erica hears her mother, she comes and stands at the door. "You can't come in," she says.

The next day the children seem cheerful and normal. They eat breakfast together. Then Suzanna says, "Don't forget. You must not talk to strangers. You must not talk to that woman. You must not take food from anyone."

Damon's face is red. "I want to talk to her. You can't stop me!"

"Yes I can," shouts Suzanna. "I'm your mother! I'm going to walk to school with you, and meet you after school, so you can't talk to her."

They take the elevator down to the street. It is cold. People are wearing thick jackets and hats and scarves.

"Maybe it will snow," says Suzanna. "That will be exciting!"

The children don't answer. They are both very angry. They go into the school and Suzanna walks home.

Suzanna walks back to the school in the afternoon. She meets the children.

"Would you like to go to the ice cream shop?" she asks.

"No, thank you," says Damon. He walks next to his mother but he doesn't talk to her. Erica is also very quiet.

*What can I do?* thinks Suzanna. They walk very fast because it is so cold.

They arrive at their apartment building. The elevator is broken.

"Oh, no!" says Suzanna. "We'll have to walk up the stairs."

"That's OK," says Erica. "The elevator smells bad. Damon and I always walk up the stairs."

Their apartment is on the fifth floor. On the third floor, Suzanna stops for a rest.

"There's the gin…" Damon hits Erica.

"Don't hit your sister," says Suzanna. Then she stops and looks at the door of one of the third floor apartments. It is painted orange-brown. But someone has painted stars and birds and flowers in bright colours all over the door and doorframe.

"Is this the gingerbread house?" she asks.

Damon kicks the wall. "Yes. It's not a gingerbread house. It's just an apartment. But Erica thinks it looks like the cottage in Hansel and Gretel."

"Have you been in that apartment?" Suzanna is very worried.

"Yes," says Damon. "A few times."

"Why do you do that?"

"The gingerbread lady invites us," says Erica. "She's nice."

"Do you ring the doorbell?" Suzanna doesn't understand.

"No," says Damon. "Sometimes when we are walking up to our apartment, the lady is going into her apartment, or coming out. Then we talk. Sometimes she invites us into the apartment. We don't stay long. I like her. She listens to me." Damon looks angrily at his mother.

They hear a strange noise from the stairs. Suzanna looks down. A very round old lady wearing a thick coat and boots and a headscarf is climbing the stairs very slowly.

She finally gets to the third floor. "Good afternoon children," she says.

She sees Suzanna. She smiles.

"Are you the mother of these lovely children?"

Suzanna doesn't answer but the old woman continues to talk. "I am Ursula Bruck. Come in, I will make coffee and hot chocolate."

Erica pulls at Suzanna's hand. "Mom, please. She's nice."

"No. Quiet, Erica!" Suzanna turns to the old woman. "Stay away from my children!"

Suzanna takes the children's hands and pulls them up the stairs.

Inside their apartment she tries to explain to the children. "New York is a big city. You have to be careful. There are many dangerous people. You can't make friends with strangers."

Damon looks at her. "If we don't talk to people, how can we make friends?"

"I will choose your friends. There are good people and bad people. You don't understand. You are too young!" shouts Suzanna.

Damon goes to his room and closes the door. Erica gets a blanket from her bedroom. She turns on the TV and lies on the sofa under the blanket. The children cannot watch TV on school nights, but Suzanna has a headache. She is too tired and upset to argue with her daughter.

The next week is difficult. It is Christmas week. Suzanna buys a Christmas tree and decorates it. She asks the children to help her make cookies. She tries hard but when Erica tastes the cookies, she says, "The gingerbread lady's cookies are better."

Suzanna walks to school with the children and goes to meet them after school every day. They always ride in the elevator. Erica doesn't like the smell.

On Christmas Eve, Suzanna takes the children to the local church. The choir is singing carols. The church is full of families. Suzanna feels lonely. She misses her husband, but the children are happier tonight. They enjoyed the carols and they are looking forward to Christmas Day.

On Christmas morning, the children come to Suzanna's bedroom very early. They jump on the bed. "We have a present for you!" says Erica.

"We have two presents," says Damon. He looks proud.

The children have made cards for Suzanna. They have drawn Christmas trees and decorated them with glitter and beads. They have written messages to her.

Erica has written: ---*Merry Christmas, best mother, love Erica*---

Damon has written: ---*Merry Christmas to the best Mom in the world*---

Suzanna starts to cry. "Thank you! These are wonderful! How did you learn to do it?"

Damon and Erica say nothing.

"Did the gingerbread lady teach you?" she asked.

"Yes," says Damon. "We said to her, 'We want to buy our mom a present because our dad is not here, and she is unhappy'."

"But we didn't have any money," says Erica. "So we couldn't buy you a present. But the gingerbread lady said 'Moms like homemade presents best'. She showed us how to make the cards and she gave us some beads."

Suzanna gets up. She makes breakfast. The children open their presents. Alan calls from Saudi Arabia. It is a very happy time. Later in the morning, Suzanna goes down to the third floor. She wants to say sorry to Ursula. She wants to invite her to lunch.

She walks down the stairs. When she gets to the third floor she is very surprised. The orange-brown door is there. But there are no beautiful painted decorations of stars and birds and flowers. It is an ordinary painted door.

Suzanna rings the doorbell. No one answers. She looks through the mailbox. The apartment seems to be empty.

She thinks it is very strange. She walks back upstairs.

Damon and Erica are playing with their Christmas presents.

"The gingerbread lady came," says Erica. "She thinks the cards we made are beautiful!"

"The gingerbread lady! But I just went down to her apartment. She isn't there! I didn't see her on the stairs!"

"No," says Erica. "I think sometimes you see her, and sometimes you don't."

"She brought these," says Damon. On the table was a box of cookies.

There is a note on top of the box.

*---Dear Suzanna. Have a nice Christmas. Best wishes, Ursula Bruck.--*

"The gingerbread lady will come and visit us next year," says Erica.

"But we will be in our new house next Christmas," says Suzanna.

Damon laughs. "That's OK. She is the gingerbread lady. She knows everything."

# 5.  A CHRISTMAS PRESENT FOR TIMMY

Walter is retired. His wife is dead, and he has no children. He lives a quiet life. But he has a job for a few days every year. He is a Santa in a big department store.

He catches a train early in the morning. He arrives at the store. It is closed, but there is a side door for the staff. He goes to the toy department. He changes into his red Santa suit. He is not a big man but Santa is fat. So he puts a pillow under his Santa suit. He wears a white beard, a long wig of white hair, a red hat and big black boots.

All day he sits in the toy department. Children come with their parents. They tell Santa what they want for Christmas. Most children want toys like video games, bikes, robots and fairy dolls.

On Christmas Eve, the store is open until late. Walter talks to children all day. He is very tired. It is 9:00pm and the store is closing. Walter is pleased. He needs a rest. He stands up. He sees a small boy and his mother. They are walking quickly towards him.

"I know it is late, but please let my son talk to you," says the woman.

The woman and the boy look tired. Their clothes are old and cheap.

Walter is tired too, but he is a kind man.

"Of course," he says in his Santa voice. "Come here and tell me what you want for Christmas."

The little boy speaks very quietly. Walter can't hear him.

"Santa is getting old. He doesn't hear so well. Come closer and tell me again," he says cheerfully.

The little boy comes very close and says, "Santa, please bring me a grandfather for Christmas."

Walter is surprised. He looks at the little boy's mother.

"Yes," she says. "Timmy wants a grandfather for Christmas."

"Why do you want a grandfather for Christmas, Timmy?" asks Walter.

"My Dad is dead. I don't want a new dad. But it's only Mom and me. It's quiet. So I would like a grandfather."

Walter is worried. Of course children don't get everything they ask for. But this little boy is so serious, and his mother looks so sad.

Then Walter has an idea.

"Santa is a little tired tonight," he says to Timmy. "I need you to help me."

"OK," says Timmy.

"I can't remember your address. If I can't find your house, I won't be able to visit you tonight. Can you write your address? Maybe your mom will help you."

The woman looks at Walter. She is surprised, but she takes a piece of paper and a pen from her bag. She helps Timmy to write their address. Timmy gives the piece of paper to Walter.

"Thank you!" says Walter. "Now go and look in the big box next to the Christmas tree. I think you will find a bag of candy there."

Timmy runs over to the tree.

"Can I be a grandfather for Timmy?" Walter asks the woman. "I have no grandchildren and my life is quiet. I would love to have a grandson. I can come and visit your house tomorrow."

The woman smiles. "I was hoping for some kind of magic for Timmy. Thank you. Yes. Please come tomorrow."

The next morning Timmy is feeling sad. There is a toy car and a bag of candy at the end of his bed, but there is no grandfather.

His mother says, "But Santa can't carry a grandfather in his sack. You have to wait."

They are eating breakfast when the doorbell rings.

"Go and answer the door," says Timmy's mother.

Timmy opens the door.

There is a white-haired man standing there. He is smiling. He is carrying two big bags.

"Good morning," he says. "Are you Timmy?"

"Yes!" says Timmy.

"Well, it's nice to meet you. I am your Christmas grandfather."

Walter spends Christmas day with Timmy and his mother.

He stays until the evening. Before he goes home, he hugs Timmy. Timmy hugs him back.

"Thank you for coming," says Timmy. "I had a grandfather for a day!"

Walter looks at Timmy's mother. "Maybe I can come again," says Walter.

Timmy's mother smiles. "Please come any time. As often as possible. Grandfathers are very special people."

# THANK YOU

Thank you for reading Christmas Tales. (Word count: 6,931) We hope you enjoyed it.

If you would like to read more Christmas stories, please see our Level 3 graded reader "Stories for Christmas".

If you would like to read more level 2 graded readers, please visit our website http://www.italkyoutalk.com

Other Level 2 graded readers include
Adventure in Rome
Andre's Dream
A Passion for Music
Danger in Seattle
Don't Come Back
Finders Keepers…
Marcy's Bakery
Men's Konkatsu Tales
Salaryman Secrets!
Stories for Halloween
The Perfect Wedding
The House in the Forest
The School on Bolt Street
Train Travel
Trouble in Paris

Women's Konkatsu Tales

# ABOUT THE AUTHOR

I Talk You Talk Press is a Japan-based publisher of language textbooks, graded readers and language learning/teaching resources.

Our team is made up of highly experienced language teachers and translators, who have all studied at least one additional language to an advanced level.

This experience enables us to design our materials from the perspective of both the teacher and the learner. We consult with both teachers and language learners when designing our textbooks and graded readers, and test our materials extensively in the classroom before publication.

We are a fast-growing press, and currently publish graded readers for learners of English. We publish new graded readers monthly.

9 784907 056865